A Prayer Book for Catholic Families

A Prayer Book

FOR

CATHOLIC FAMILIES

LOYOLAPRESS.

CHICAGO

LOYOLAPRESS.

3441 N. ASHLAND AVENUE
CHICAGO, ILLINOIS 60657
(800) 621-1008
WWW.LOYOLABOOKS.ORG

Some of the prayers and commentary originally appeared in *A Prayer Primer for Catholic Families,* © 1997 Loyola Press.

Copyright acknowledgments appear on pages 165-168 and constitute a continuation of this copyright page.

Cover design by Tracey Sainz
Cover art by Susan Tolonen
Interior design by Kathryn Seckman Kirsch
Interior art by Susan Tolonen

Library of Congress Cataloging-in-Publication Data
A prayer book for Catholic families / [edited by Christopher Anderson,
    Susan Gleason Anderson, and LaVonne Neff].
        p.   cm.
    Includes bibliographical references and index.
    ISBN 0-8294-1528-9
    1. Catholic Church—Prayer-books and devotions—English.
2. Family—Prayer-books and devotions—English.   I. Anderson,
Christopher.   II. Anderson, Susan Gleason.   III. Neff, LaVonne.
BX2170.F3P73   1998
242'.802—dc21   97-49896
                                                                    CIP

First revised edition printing, March 2008
revised edition ISBN-13: 978-0-8294-2717-2
                    ISBN-10: 0-8294-2717-1

Printed in the United States of America
08 09 10 11 12 13 Versa 10 9 8 7 6 5 4 3 2 1

Contents

three

four

five

MORNING AND EVENING PRAYER | 59

six

seven

DEVOTIONS TO MARY | 121

eight

THE COMMUNION OF SAINTS | 147

nine

one

A Tradition of Family Prayer

F<small>OR MOST OF US, OUR INTRODUCTION TO FAITH CAME FROM FAMILY MEMBERS.</small> Our fathers and mothers, brothers and sisters, grandparents, aunts, and uncles helped shape our physical, emotional, intellectual, and social development. They also played a major role in our spiritual formation. And now that we are adults, we in turn are influencing the spiritual lives of our younger siblings, our nieces and nephews, and—especially—our children.

The Catholic Church recognizes and affirms this primary place of the family in religious formation. Documents of the Second Vatican Council called the family "the domestic church." In the family, new Christians are born, and young people have their first experiences of God.

If faith begins in the family, so does prayer. Prayer expresses the faith we already have. It helps our faith to grow and mature. As we relate with our family members day by day, we can be learning how to relate with God through prayer.

Many Ways to Pray

Prayer can be described in various ways:

- Prayer is the lifting of the mind, heart, and will to God.
- Prayer is conversation with God, both speaking and listening.
- Prayer is a gift that enables us to have a relationship with the One who is our Creator, Redeemer, and God.
- Prayer helps to form our faith. An ancient maxim of the Church teaches us: *As we pray, so we believe.* And our daily experience shows us that as we believe, so we act. Prayer turns us into the people we pray to become.

Vocal prayer—prayer that is spoken aloud—is only one of many forms of prayer. Some prayers are spoken silently, in the heart. Some prayers use no words at all. When we pray aloud, we may express our concerns in our own words. We may praise God in song or poetry. Or we may use prayer structures like the ones in this book. They cover the spectrum of prayer: blessing, petition, intercession, thanksgiving, and praise. A taste of each in your daily prayer will provide well-rounded nourishment for your spirit.

Using Prayer Models

Prayer, of course, is much more than the structure we learned as children. But structures—prayer models—are an excellent way to learn to pray. When Jesus' disciples came to him and said, "Lord, teach us to pray," he gave them the words of the Lord's Prayer. Throughout Christian history, this prayer has been the classic model for Christian prayer.

Prayer models give us time-honored words that have helped to shape the Christian community. As we repeat the words, we join Christians from all ages and all places. We come to God with Middle Eastern fishermen of two thousand years ago, the fourth-century African bishop St. Augustine, the fifteenth-century warrior St. Joan, Mother Teresa of Calcutta, and our own great-grandparents, as well as the people with whom we live, work, study, play, and go to church.

Prayer models express the community's identity and the way we worship God together. Favorite prayer models also express a family's identity and help to create an atmosphere of faith.

Beginning a Tradition

A Prayer Book for Catholic Families is a book of prayer models that are the heritage of every Catholic—prayers for holy days and ordinary days; prayers of blessing and contrition, sorrow and rejoicing, petition and thanksgiving. It is a book to dip into when you want a prayer for a special occasion, a book to refer to when your memory needs jogging about a familiar prayer, a book to use daily if you want to gather your family for morning or evening prayers. It is not an encyclopedic collection of every prayer known to the Church, but a practical book you can keep close at hand.

This book was designed for hard use. It is small, so little hands and hands that have lost their strength can hold it. The Contents page at the front of the book, the section tabs, and the list of prayers at the end can help you quickly find the right prayer for every need. There is even space to add your own favorite Scripture passage or prayer.

This is not just a pretty book to look at and put on a shelf. It is a tool to help your family—parents and children, grandparents and guests—pray together.

A Time and a Place

Creating a family prayer life is an important responsibility. It means making time and space for prayer—admittedly, not easy to do in today's busy society with so many competing activities. Yet this busyness may make it even more important for families to find time to pray together.

Mealtime graces and bedtime blessings are remembered long after children grow up, leave home, and have children of their own. Many families also make time for more extended prayers, often just before or just after dinner while the family is still at the table.

Choose a time and place that fit for your family to pray together, and keep this book nearby—on the dinner table or a nightstand or within reach of your most comfortable sofa. If you have a family Bible, you may wish to keep that on hand, too. This book uses the New Revised Standard Version, but any Catholic Bible translation you prefer is fine.

Then, when prayer time comes, you'll be ready.

Praying with Children

Even the youngest children can be part of family prayer. They can learn to hold hands and to be quietly attentive during grace and bedtime prayers. The first prayer children should learn is just one word—they can say "amen" after prayers led by others.

As children grow, they can take a greater role in family prayer life. Build their interest by giving them parts to say and tasks to perform, such as bringing the prayer book or lighting a candle.

As they begin school, they should begin learning the common prayers of the Catholic tradition. Teach them the Sign of the Cross, the Lord's Prayer, and the Hail Mary, as well as the responses said at Mass. Don't wait for them to learn these prayers at church or as a school assignment. Introduce them in the context of your own family prayer times.

Older children can choose prayers, lead prayers, or make up prayers of their own. They may want to sing, meditate, listen to a recording, or discuss their intentions. Variety in prayer will help keep children interested and, at the same time, broaden their faith experience.

While it is natural for junior high and high school-aged children to be reluctant to join in family prayer, continue to invite them. They should feel welcome not only by your words but also by the beauty and power of the experience. And at times, adults should let children have their space. Even when children choose not to participate, they will draw strength from their experience of the family as a praying community.

Lifelong Blessings

Praying families make lasting impressions on all their members. Though children grow up and leave home, they never forget the faith environment of their earliest years. We hope that this collection of prayers will help you and your family to discover the rich heritage of Catholic prayer and, as you pray together, to recognize God's presence within your ordinary family life. We pray that for you and your family, prayer will become a lifelong resource and blessing.

two

FAVORITE PRAYERS

HERE ARE PRAYERS FOR THOSE JUST LEARNING TO PRAY—THE VERY YOUNG, THOSE NEW TO THE FAITH—AS WELL AS FOR THOSE WHO HAVE PRAYED ALL THROUGH THEIR LIVES. These familiar prayers are the tradition of all Catholic Christians, as ancient as the faith itself and as new as the faith we bring to each new day.

Amen

The word "amen" means "truly" or "certainly" or, simply, "yes." Ancient Hebrews and Greek-speaking Christians ended their prayers with this hearty affirmation, just as we do today. When we say "amen" at the end of a prayer, we add our agreement to everything in the prayer. "Amen" can be the first prayer of a small child, the last prayer of a dying person, and the only prayer of a person whose body, mind, or soul is weak. It is a prayer of the heart.

Amen!

The Sign of the Cross

The most basic prayer in the Catholic Christian tradition is the sign of the cross. We often begin our prayers and our liturgy by tracing the shape of the cross on our bodies while speaking the names of the Trinity. Whenever we make the sign of the cross, we recall our baptism, because it was at our baptism that we were first marked with the sign of the cross and claimed for Christ. The words of this prayer confess our faith in God as Trinity, and thus the prayer is a kind of creed. It is also used frequently as a blessing ritual, and it is common to speak of making the sign of the cross as "blessing oneself."

In the name of the Father, and of the Son, and of the Holy Spirit.
Amen.

The Doxology

In these few lines, we express our faith in God's Trinity (that the one-and-only God exists in three Persons) and eternity (that God has no beginning or end). The Doxology, a Greek word meaning "words of praise," is often used in prayer services and devotions, especially in the Rosary and in Morning and Evening Prayer.

Glory be to the Father,
and to the Son,
and to the Holy Spirit.
As it was in the beginning,
is now, and ever shall be,
world without end.
Amen.

The Lord's Prayer

The Lord's Prayer, or the Our Father, is the prayer Jesus gave his disciples when they asked him to teach them to pray (see Luke 11:1–4 and Matthew 6:9–15). For twenty centuries, Christians have used this prayer as a model.

More than seven hundred years ago, St. Thomas Aquinas wrote in his *Summa Theologica*: "The Lord's Prayer is the most perfect of prayers. . . . In it we ask, not only for all the things we can rightly desire, but also in the sequence that they should be desired. This prayer not only teaches us to ask for things, but also in what order we should desire them."[1] (II-II 83, 9) Look at the sequence of requests and praises, line by line. What does the Lord's Prayer teach us about how to pray?

Our Father, who art in heaven,
hallowed be thy name;
thy kingdom come;
thy will be done
on earth as it is in heaven.
Give us this day our daily bread;
and forgive us our trespasses
as we forgive those who trespass against us;
and lead us not into temptation,
but deliver us from evil.
Amen.

The following doxology (praise) is frequently added to the Lord's Prayer. It is not in the scriptural texts, but Christians have prayed it from the earliest days of the Church. We recite it when we pray the Lord's Prayer during Mass.

For the kingdom, the power and the glory are yours, now
and for ever.
Amen.

The Apostles' Creed

No one knows when or where this creed was first used, though it was probably several centuries after the apostles' time. Whatever its historical origins, it expresses the most important truths about the nature of God that Catholics hold. When we say the Apostles' Creed, we affirm our belief in God as Trinity: Father, Son, and Holy Spirit. The Apostles' Creed is used in personal prayer, devotions, and some liturgical settings. It is most widely said during the Rosary and at children's Masses. The Nicene Creed is the one you typically pray at Mass; it can be found on Page 46.

I believe in God, the Father almighty,
    creator of heaven and earth.
I believe in Jesus Christ, his only Son, our Lord.
    He was conceived by the power of
            the Holy Spirit
        and born of the Virgin Mary.
    He suffered under Pontius Pilate,
        was crucified, died, and was buried.
    He descended to the dead.
    On the third day he arose again.
    He ascended into heaven,
        and is seated at the right hand of the Father.
    He will come again to judge the living
            and the dead.
I believe in the Holy Spirit,
    the holy catholic Church,
    the communion of saints,
    the forgiveness of sins,
    the resurrection of the body,
    and the life everlasting.
Amen.

Prayer to the Holy Spirit

When we pray, we usually address God the Father or God the Son (Jesus). But because each person of the Trinity is equally God, it is also possible to address our prayer to the Holy Spirit, as does this ancient prayer.

LEADER:

Come, Holy Spirit, fill the hearts of your faithful.

ALL:

And kindle in them the fire of your love.

LEADER:

Send forth your Spirit and they shall be created.

ALL:

And you will renew the face of the earth.

LEADER:

Let us pray.

Lord,
by the light of the Holy Spirit
you have taught the hearts of your faithful.
In the same Spirit
help us to relish what is right
and always rejoice in your consolation.
We ask this through Christ our Lord.

ALL:

Amen.[2]

Anima Christi

This prayer comes from the early fourteenth century. It was used during private devotions to the Eucharist. The author is unknown, but St. Ignatius of Loyola knew the prayer and recommended it in his *Spiritual Exercises*. The title of the prayer is Latin for "Soul of Christ."

Soul of Christ, sanctify me.
Body of Christ, heal me.
Blood of Christ, drench me.
Water from the side of Christ, wash me.
Passion of Christ, strengthen me.

Good Jesus, hear me.

In your wounds shelter me.
From turning away, keep me.
From the evil one protect me.
At the hour of my death call me.
Into your presence lead me,
to praise you with all your saints
for ever and ever.
Amen.[3]

The Three Theological Virtues

In Catholic teaching, three virtues are identified as gifts from God: faith, hope, and love. These are called the theological virtues, and they are listed together in Paul's First Letter to the Corinthians (13:13). All other human virtues are rooted in these three. The following prayers focus on each of the theological virtues.

Act of Faith

O my God, I firmly believe that you are one God
in three divine Persons, Father, Son, and Holy Spirit.
I believe that your divine Son became man and died for
*   our sins,*
and that he will come to judge the living and the dead.
I believe these and all the truths
which the holy Catholic Church teaches,
because you have revealed them,
who can neither deceive nor be deceived. Amen.

Act of Hope

O my God, relying on your infinite mercy and promises,
I hope to obtain pardon of my sins, the help of your grace,
and life everlasting, through the merits of Jesus Christ,
my Lord and Redeemer. Amen.

Act of Love

O my God, I love you above all things
with my whole heart and soul, because you are all good
and worthy of all my love.
I love my neighbor as myself for the love of you.
I forgive all who have injured me
and I ask pardon of those whom I have injured. Amen.

Vocation Prayer

Although the word "vocation" is most frequently associated with religious vocations to the priesthood or to religious life, every state of life is really a vocation, or a calling. Married life, single life, and religious life are all Christian vocations. It is part of Catholic tradition to pray for God's guidance to help us find the way of life to which God is calling us.

Lord, let me know clearly
the work which you are calling me to do in life.
And grant me every grace I need to answer your call
with courage and love and lasting dedication
to your will.
Amen.

To the Guardian Angel

According to popular Catholic belief, each person has a special angel who watches over him or her. Though this widespread belief has never been a part of official church teachings, guardian angels are honored on October 2. Here is a traditional prayer:

Angel sent by God to guide me,
be my light and walk beside me;
be my guardian and protect me;
in the paths of life direct me.
Amen.

three

BLESSINGS AND GRACES

CATHOLICS LOVE BLESSINGS. Our most basic blessing is the sign of the cross, with which we bless ourselves and our loved ones. But there are many and more elaborate means by which we invite God's favor. Prayers of blessing appear throughout scripture. There is an entire book of liturgical blessings offered by the Church for various people and occasions. In addition, prayers of blessing are used to consecrate objects and spaces for sacred use.

We may ask priests to bless us, but the act of blessing is not reserved for the priesthood. In the baptismal rite, parents and godparents are invited to mark the child to be baptized with the sign of the cross. This can be the first of many opportunities for parents to invite God's favor on their children. Some parents bless their children regularly—at bedtime, at mealtimes, or whenever children leave the house.

The blessing of and giving thanks for food is an important aspect not just of Catholicism, but of all religious traditions. Mention of the practice can be found in both the Old and New Testaments. When we bless our food, we stop and remember that all good things come from God. We ask God's blessing on the food and all those gathered to share it.

The act of blessing can be elaborate or simple. Sometimes it makes use of sacramentals, such as holy water. Sometimes the ritual includes only prayer and gesture. Here are some prayers of blessing to serve as models for your family.

Moses' Blessing of the Israelites

The LORD bless you and keep you;
the LORD make his face to shine upon you,
    and be gracious to you;
the LORD lift up his countenance upon you,
    and give you peace.

NUMBERS 6:24–26

Jacob's Blessing of Isaac

May God give you of the dew of heaven,
and of the fatness of the earth,
and plenty of grain and wine.

GENESIS 27:28

A Blessing with Children

The parents say:

Father,
inexhaustible source of life and author of all good,
we bless you and we thank you
for brightening our communion of love by your
gift of children.
Grant that our children [child] will find in the life
of this family such inspiration
that they [he/she] will strive always for what is
right and good
and one day, by your grace,
reach their [his/her] home in heaven.

We ask this through Christ our Lord.
Amen.

The children respond, while making the sign of the cross:

May the Lord Jesus, who loved children,
bless us and keep us in his love,
now and for ever.
Amen.[4]

A Blessing of Children

May the Lord keep you
and make you grow in his love,
so that you may live worthy of the calling
*   he has given you,*
now and for ever.
Amen.[5]

A Birthday Blessing for an Adult

Loving God, source of all life,
We give you thanks for the gift of life you have given us.
Hear the prayers of [Name]
Who today celebrates the day of his/her birth
And the gift of life that he/she shares
With family and friends.
Surrounded with your loving presence,
May he/she enjoy many more years
To praise you
And to share your love with others.
Grant this through Christ our Lord.
Amen.

A Birthday Blessing for a Child

Loving God,
You have created each of us
And enfold us in your love.
You have called us each by name
And constantly care for us.
Look with favor on your child, [Name],
Who begins another year of life.
Bless him/her with the joy of your love and friendship.
Give him/her the strength of your grace
That he/she may share your love with family and friends
Throughout the coming year.
We ask this through Christ our Lord.
Amen.

A Blessing for a Sick Child

Father of mercy and God of all consolation,
you show tender care for all your creatures
and give health of soul and body.
Raise up this child from his [her] sickness.
Then, growing in wisdom and grace in your
*   sight and ours,*
he [she] will serve you all the days of his [her] life
in uprightness and holiness
and offer the thanksgiving due to your mercy.

We ask this through Christ our Lord.
Amen.[6]

Mealtime Prayers

Pausing before we pick up our forks offers a moment to acknowledge our togetherness. This time is precious in unifying our family and bringing an awareness of God's presence to our table.

We might always say the traditional prayer. In doing so, we are also unified with our larger family, the Catholic Church, whose members have uttered the same or similar phrases for years upon years.

But if prayer becomes habit over heart, there are ways to be more mindful at mealtime. You could sing the traditional prayer—let your child improvise the melody. Read a poem or Scripture passage that gives thanks to God. Take turns offering your own words of gratitude before eating. Instead of—or in addition to—a prayer before meals, try a prayer after meals. Institute a moment of silence. Even that gesture can calm our spirits and reframe our focus: on each other, and on Jesus who offers us the greatest nourishment, his Body and Blood.

Grace Before Meals

The leader makes the sign of the cross and says these words:

Bless us, O Lord, and these your gifts
which we are about to receive from your bounty.
Through Christ our Lord.
Amen.

Or the leader says:

In peace let us pray to the Lord.
Let each of us be mindful
of all that we have received from his hands
and for which we give thanks:
food, family, friends,
work, health, and happy memories.

(Pause for silent prayer.)

In giving thanks we are blessed.
Amen.

Grace After Meals

We give you thanks
for all your gifts,
almighty God,
living and reigning
now and for ever.
Amen.

A Prayer of Thanksgiving

This psalm of praise makes a lovely table grace either before or after meals.

May God be gracious to us and bless us
and make his face to shine upon us.
The earth has yielded its increase;
God, our God, has blessed us.
May God continue to bless us;
let all the ends of the earth revere him.
FROM PSALM 67:2, 7–8

We thank you for your gifts, merciful God,
and we ask you to give all people the food they need.
May we all be united one day

in the eternal singing of your praises,
through Christ, our Lord.
Amen.

four

PRAYERS WE SAY AT MASS

AFTER YEARS OF ATTENDING MASS, WE KNOW CERTAIN PRAYERS BY HEART. We may not remember where we first heard them or how we learned them, but they are a permanent part of our Catholic tradition. Children enjoy learning these prayers and saying them along with the grown-ups at Mass. And these prayers do not have to be reserved for Sundays. They are beautiful prayers for any time, any place.[7]

The Order of the Mass

The Mass is the high point of our faith life as Catholics. It always follows a set order.

Introductory Rites

We gather as a community to celebrate God's presence in our lives. We praise God together in song during the Entrance Procession and pray the sign of the cross.

The Sign of the Cross

In the name of the Father,
and of the Son,
and of the Holy Spirit.
Amen.

The greeting follows:

PRIEST: *The grace of our Lord Jesus Christ and the love of God and the fellowship of the Holy Spirit be with you all.*
PEOPLE: *And also with you.*

Confiteor

Our sins and mistakes are not private affairs. They affect the whole family, the entire community. That is why we confess them to our brothers and sisters—at home or at church—as well as to God.

I confess to almighty God
and to you, my brothers and sisters,
that I have sinned through my own fault,
in my thoughts and in my words,
in what I have done,
and in what I have failed to do.
And I ask blessed Mary, ever virgin,
all the angels and saints,
and you, my brothers and sisters,
to pray for me to the Lord our God.

Kyrie

Then we pray for God's mercy and forgiveness:

PRIEST: *Lord, have mercy.*

PEOPLE: *Lord, have mercy.*

PRIEST: *Christ, have mercy.*

PEOPLE: *Christ, have mercy.*

PRIEST: *Lord, have mercy.*

PEOPLE: *Lord, have mercy.*

PRIEST: *May almighty God have mercy on us, forgive us our sins, and bring us to everlasting life.*

PEOPLE: *Amen.*

Gloria

This ancient hymn of praise begins with the words of the angels who sang to shepherds in the hills of Bethlehem when Christ was born.

Glory to God in the highest,
and peace to his people on earth.
Lord God, heavenly King,
almighty God and Father,
we worship you, we give you thanks,
we praise you for your glory.
Lord Jesus Christ, only Son of the Father,
Lord God, Lamb of God,
you take away the sin of the world:
have mercy on us;
you are seated at the right hand of the Father:
receive our prayer.
For you alone are the Holy One,
you alone are the Lord,
you alone are the Most High,
Jesus Christ,
with the Holy Spirit,
in the glory of God the Father. Amen.

Collect

We ask God to hear our prayers. First, we all pray in silence. Then the priest prays aloud and we respond "Amen."

Liturgy of the Word

We listen to God's Word proclaimed from Sacred Scripture in the Liturgy of the Word. This part of the Mass includes the priest's homily, our profession of faith, and our prayers of petition to God.

First Reading

This is usually from the Old Testament or the Acts of the Apostles. We respond:

LECTOR: *The Word of the Lord.*
PEOPLE: *Thanks be to God.*

Responsorial Psalm

The lector or the cantor invites us to pray the words of the Psalm, usually in song.

Second Reading

We hear from the books of the New Testament: one of the Letters or the Book of Revelation. We respond again:

LECTOR: *The Word of the Lord.*
PEOPLE: *Thanks be to God.*

Gospel

We stand and, except during Lent, we sing "Alleluia!" to praise God for the Good News we will hear in the Gospel.

PRIEST OR DEACON: *The Lord be with you.*
PEOPLE: *And also with you.*
PRIEST OR DEACON: *A reading from the holy Gospel according to . . .*
PEOPLE: *Glory to you, Lord.*

Then everyone traces a cross on their foreheads, lips, and hearts. We pray that God's Word will be in our minds, on our lips, and in our hearts.

After the priest or deacon proclaims the Gospel, we respond:

PRIEST OR DEACON: *The Gospel of the Lord.*
PEOPLE: *Praise to you, Lord Jesus Christ.*

Homily

We then sit and listen as the priest or deacon explains how we can live out God's Word.

The Nicene Creed

Throughout the history of the Church, Christians have professed their faith by learning and reciting creeds—summary statements that express the beliefs of the whole community. The Nicene Creed, whose roots are more than sixteen hundred years old, describes the God we worship. We can pray it as an expression of faith and praise.

We believe in one God,
*   the Father, the Almighty,*
*   maker of heaven and earth,*
*   of all that is seen and unseen.*
We believe in one Lord, Jesus Christ,
*   the only Son of God,*
*   eternally begotten of the Father,*
*   God from God, Light from Light,*
*   true God from true God,*
*   begotten, not made, one in Being with the Father.*
*   Through him all things were made.*
*   For us men and for our salvation*
*   he came down from heaven:*

(bow your heads as you pray the next phrase)
by the power of the Holy Spirit

he was born of the Virgin Mary, and became man.
For our sake he was crucified under Pontius Pilate;
he suffered, died, and was buried.
On the third day he rose again
in fulfillment of the Scriptures;
he ascended into heaven
and is seated at the right hand of the Father.
He will come again in glory to judge the living and
the dead,
and his kingdom will have no end.
We believe in the Holy Spirit, the Lord, the giver of life,
who proceeds from the Father and the Son.
With the Father and the Son he is worshiped
and glorified.
He has spoken through the Prophets.
We believe in one holy catholic and apostolic Church.
We acknowledge one baptism for the forgiveness
of sins.
We look for the resurrection of the dead,
and the life of the world to come. Amen.

Prayer of the Faithful

We ask God to hear our prayers for the Church, for the world, for people in need, and for ourselves.

Liturgy of the Eucharist

During the Liturgy of the Eucharist, we offer ourselves together with the gifts of bread and wine. The Eucharistic Prayer is our prayer of thanksgiving. Jesus' sacrifice on the cross is made present again, and Jesus himself is present with us. The bread and the wine become the Body and Blood of Jesus Christ. We receive this most precious gift in Holy Communion.

Preparation of the Gifts

Gifts of bread and wine are brought to the altar.

The priest lifts up the bread and prays a prayer, sometimes aloud. We respond "Blessed be God for ever."

Then he raises the wine and says a prayer, sometimes aloud. We respond the same way.

We stand as the priest prays over the gifts. He asks God to accept our sacrifice.

PRIEST: *Pray, my brothers and sisters, that our sacrifice*
may be acceptable to God, the almighty Father.

PEOPLE: *May the Lord accept the sacrifice at your hands*
for the praise and glory of his name, for our
good, and the good of all his Church. Amen.

Eucharistic Prayer

This prayer of thanksgiving is the center and high point
of the entire celebration. In the Preface, the priest invites
us to give thanks and praise to God.

PRIEST: *The Lord be with you.*

PEOPLE: *And also with you.*

PRIEST: *Lift up your hearts.*

PEOPLE: *We lift them up to the Lord.*

PRIEST: *Let us give thanks to the Lord our God.*

PEOPLE: *It is right to give him thanks and praise.*

Sanctus

One of the oldest Christian prayers, the Sanctus reminds us of the people who spread palm branches before Jesus as he rode into Jerusalem on the back of a donkey. "Hosanna!"—"Save us!"—they called out to him. The threefold repetition of "Holy" is in honor of the Trinity.

Holy, holy, holy Lord, God of power and might,
heaven and earth are full of your glory.
　　Hosanna in the highest.
Blessed is he who comes in the name of the Lord.
　　Hosanna in the highest.

Consecration

We kneel during the part of the Eucharistic Prayer that follows the Sanctus. During the consecration, the priest prays the words that Jesus spoke at the Last Supper. Through the power of the Holy Spirit and the words and actions of the priest, the bread and wine become the Body and Blood of Jesus Christ.

Memorial Acclamation

After the priest has consecrated the bread and wine, we all together affirm our faith in Christ's death, resurrection, and second coming. These short creeds can be prayed whenever we feel the need for added strength and courage.

A

Christ has died,
Christ is risen,
Christ will come again.

B

Dying you destroyed our death,
rising you restored our life.
Lord Jesus, come in glory.

C

When we eat this bread and drink this cup,
we proclaim your death, Lord Jesus,
until you come in glory.

D

Lord, by your cross and resurrection
you have set us free.
You are the Savior of the world.

The priest continues to pray the words of the Eucharistic Prayer, asking God to receive our sacrifice of praise. He joins our prayer with the prayers of the whole Church. Then the priest prays the Final Doxology and the Great Amen. When we pray Amen, we are saying "yes" in faith to all that we have prayed in the Eucharistic Prayer.

PRIEST: *Through him,*
With him,
In him,
In the unity of the Holy Spirit,
> *All glory and honor is yours,*
> *Almighty Father,*
> *For ever and ever.*
PEOPLE: *Amen.*

Communion Rite

Now we prepare to receive the Body and Blood of Jesus Christ. We pray to be united with one another in Christ. We stand and pray together the Lord's Prayer.

Our Father, who art in heaven,
hallowed be thy name;
thy kingdom come;
thy will be done
on earth as it is in heaven.
Give us this day our daily bread;
and forgive us our trespasses
as we forgive those who trespass
against us;
and lead us not into temptation,
but deliver us from evil.
Amen.

Rite of Peace

After the Lord's Prayer, the priest prays that we will be united with one another in Christ's peace.

PRIEST: *The peace of the Lord be with you always.*
PEOPLE: *And also with you.*

Then the priest or deacon invites us to offer a sign of peace to those around us. We shake hands with one another. We exchange a greeting of peace, such as, "The peace of the Lord be with you always." And we respond to one another, "Amen" or "And also with you."

The priest breaks the consecrated host.

Agnus Dei

Often set to music, this prayer is addressed to Jesus the Lamb, the sacrifice whose death brings peace to the world.

Lamb of God, you take away the sins of the world:
*   have mercy on us.*
Lamb of God, you take away the sins of the world:
*   have mercy on us.*
Lamb of God, you take away the sins of the world:
*   grant us peace.*

Communion

We kneel as we prepare to receive Holy Communion. The priest raises the consecrated host and the chalice with the consecrated wine as he prays:

PRIEST: *This is the Lamb of God who takes away the sins of the world. Happy are those who are called to his supper.*

PEOPLE: *Lord, I am not worthy to receive you, but only say the word and I shall be healed.*

Communion Procession

We receive Holy Communion from a priest, a deacon, or an extraordinary minister of Holy Communion. We receive the Body of Christ—under the form of bread—in our hands or on our tongue.

PRIEST: *The Body of Christ.*

PEOPLE: *Amen.*

We receive the Blood of Christ under the form of wine.

PRIEST: *The Blood of Christ.*

PEOPLE: *Amen.*

After we receive Holy Communion, we return to our place to thank Jesus for the gift of himself in the Eucharist. The priest invites us to stand and leads the Prayer After Communion. We ask God to help us live as Jesus has called us to live.

Concluding Rites

We continue standing as the priest invites us to pray.

PRIEST: *The Lord be with you.*
PEOPLE: *And also with you.*

The priest offers the Final Blessing.

PRIEST: *May almighty God bless you, the Father, and the Son, and the Holy Spirit.*
PEOPLE: *Amen.*

In the Dismissal, we are sent to love and serve the Lord and one another, to continue the mission given to us at Mass.

PRIEST OR DEACON: *Go in peace to love and serve the Lord.*
PEOPLE: *Thanks be to God.*

Family Favorites

A place for our favorite Scripture passages,
prayers, notes and quotes

....

....

....

....

....

....

....

....

....

....

....

....

....

....

....

....

....

....

....

....

five

MORNING AND EVENING PRAYER

MARKING THE TIME OF DAY WITH PRAYER IS AN ANCIENT TRADITION IN THE CHURCH. For centuries, monastic communities have prayed the Divine Office, also known as the Liturgy of the Hours, which focuses on praising God through psalms, canticles (short hymns that appear within scriptural texts), intercessions, and the Lord's Prayer. "The laity, too, are encouraged to recite the Divine Office, either with the priests, or among themselves, or even individually," the Constitution on the Sacred Liturgy says.

The problem for many of us is that the Divine Office is complicated. It involves singing all the psalms once each month, reading major portions of scripture each year, and meditating on inspirational writings by the saints. The full form of the Liturgy of the Hours requires several volumes of prayers, readings, and instructions. Most families don't have time for that.

But if your family would like to try Morning and Evening Prayer, there is a model you can follow. It is based on Sunday of Week I of the Four-Week Psalter. Once you're comfortable with the rhythm, you may want to buy a more complete form of the Divine Office, such as *Shorter Christian Prayer* (New York: Catholic Book Publishing Co., 1988), from which these prayers were taken.

Pray as much of Morning and Evening Prayers as you can, as often as you can. Don't worry if you don't have time for all the prayers, or if you can only complete them on weekends. The important thing is turning your thoughts and hearts to God regularly.

Morning Prayer

Morning prayer is a wonderful way to get acquainted with the Liturgy of the Hours. Here is a simple form of Morning Prayer that families or individuals can use.

Opening Prayer

God, come to my assistance.
—Lord, make haste to help me.

Glory to the Father, and to the Son, and to the
*   Holy Spirit:*
as it was in the beginning, is now, and will be
*   for ever. Amen. Alleluia.*[8]

As morning breaks I look to you, O God, to be my strength
this day, alleluia.[9]

Psalm

A psalm is a song, and this is a lovely song to greet the day. After you know it well, you may wish to substitute other psalms. One person can read the entire psalm, or two people (or groups) can read alternate lines. If you choose to read alternate lines, notice how the second line usually repeats or completes the thought expressed in the first line. This repetition is typical of Hebrew songs and poems.

O God, you are my God, I seek you,
my soul thirsts for you;
my flesh faints for you,
as in a dry and weary land where there is
no water.
So I have looked upon you in the sanctuary,
beholding your power and glory.
Because your steadfast love is better than life,
my lips will praise you.
So I will bless you as long as I live;
I will lift up my hands and call on your name.
My soul is satisfied as with a rich feast,
and my mouth praises you with joyful lips

when I think of you on my bed,

    and meditate on you in the watches of the night;
for you have been my help,

    and in the shadow of your wings I sing for joy.
My soul clings to you;

    your right hand upholds me.

PSALM 63:1–8

Glory be to the Father,
and to the Son,
and to the Holy Spirit.
As it was in the beginning,
is now, and ever shall be,
world without end.
Amen.

Psalm-prayer

Father, creator of unfailing light, give that same light to those who call to you. May our lips praise you; our lives proclaim your goodness; our works give you honor, and our voices celebrate you for ever.[10]

A Reading from Scripture

Next, read a short passage of scripture of your choice. Some families use the daily readings (you can find them in a weekday missal or possibly in your parish bulletin), and some choose a book of the Bible to read straight through, a paragraph or two a day. Children often prefer the books of scripture that tell stories, including:

The Book of Genesis
The Book of Ruth
The Book of Judith
The Book of Esther
The Book of Daniel
The Gospel according to Matthew
The Gospel according to Mark
The Gospel according to Luke
The Gospel according to John
The Acts of the Apostles

Family Favorites

A place for our favorite Scripture passages,
prayers, notes and quotes

....

....

....

....

....

....

....

....

....

....

....

....

....

....

....

....

....

....

The Canticle of Zechariah

Follow your scripture reading with the prayer of the priest Zechariah at the birth of his son, John, known as John the Baptist.

Blessed be the Lord, the God of Israel;
he has come to his people and set them free.

He has raised up for us a mighty savior,
born of the house of his servant David.

Through his holy prophets he promised of old
that he would save us from our enemies,
from the hands of all who hate us.

He promised to show mercy to our fathers
and to remember his holy covenant.

This was the oath he swore to our father Abraham:
to set us free from the hands of our enemies,
free to worship him without fear,
holy and righteous in his sight
all the days of our life.

You, my child, shall be called the prophet of the
          Most High;
for you will go before the Lord to prepare his way,
to give his people knowledge of salvation
by the forgiveness of their sins.

In the tender compassion of our God
the dawn from on high shall break upon us,
to shine on those who dwell in darkness and the
          shadow of death,
and to guide our feet into the way of peace.[11]

Intercessions

Family members next can share their prayer intentions. After each spoken concern, the family says:

Lord, hear our prayer.

When all have had a chance to pray, the family prays together:

Our Father, who art in heaven,
hallowed be thy name;
thy kingdom come;
thy will be done
on earth as it is in heaven.
Give us this day our daily bread;
and forgive us our trespasses
as we forgive those who trespass against us;
and lead us not into temptation,
but deliver us from evil.
Amen.

Closing Prayer and Blessing

The family says together:

Almighty and ever-present Father,
your watchful care reaches from end to end
and orders all things in such power
that even the tensions and the tragedies of sin
cannot frustrate your loving plans.
Help us to embrace your will,
give us the strength to follow your call,
so that your truth may live in our hearts
and reflect peace to those who believe in your love.
We ask this in the name of Jesus the Lord.

The leader says, as all make the sign of the cross:

May the Lord bless us,
protect us from all evil
and bring us to everlasting life.
Amen.[12]

Evening Prayer

Right after dinner or just before bedtime, your family can gather and turn their thoughts toward God.

Opening Prayer

God, come to my assistance.
—Lord, make haste to help me.
Glory to the Father, and to the Son, and to the
*   Holy Spirit:*
as it was in the beginning, is now, and will be
*   for ever. Amen. Alleluia.[13]*

Like burning incense, Lord, let my prayer rise up
to you.[14]

Psalm

At the end of a busy day, this psalm, or song, is a wonderful way to express our trust in God. Read it in unison or divide into two groups and read alternate lines. After you know it well, you may wish to substitute other psalms.

I call upon you, O LORD; come quickly to me;
*   give ear to my voice when I call to you.*

Let my prayer be counted as incense before you,
*   and the lifting up of my hands as an evening*
*   sacrifice.*

Set a guard over my mouth, O Lord;
*   keep watch over the door of my lips.*
Do not turn my heart to any evil,
*   to busy myself with wicked deeds*
in company with those who work iniquity;
*   do not let me eat of their delicacies.*

But my eyes are turned toward you, O GOD, my Lord;
in you I seek refuge; do not leave me defenseless.
PSALM 141:1–4, 8

Glory be to the Father,
and to the Son,
and to the Holy Spirit.
As it was in the beginning,
is now, and ever shall be,
world without end.
Amen.

Psalm-prayer

Lord, from the rising of the sun to its setting your name is worthy of all praise. Let our prayer come like incense before you. May the lifting up of our hands be as an evening sacrifice acceptable to you, Lord our God.[15]

A Reading from Scripture

Next read a short passage of scripture of your choice. Some families use the daily readings (you can find them in a weekday missal or possibly in your parish bulletin) and some choose favorite selections, such as:

Isaiah 40: "Comfort, O comfort my people"
Isaiah 55: "Come to the waters"
John 5:22–47: The Bread from Heaven
John 14: "Do not let your hearts be troubled"
Romans 8:31–39: God's Love for Us
1 Corinthians 13: The Love Chapter

The Canticle of Mary

When Mary learned she would be the mother of our Lord, she went to visit her relative Elizabeth, who was soon to become the mother of John the Baptist. This song of praise, also known as the Magnificat, is Mary's response to Elizabeth's greeting.

My soul proclaims the greatness of the Lord,
my spirit rejoices in God my Savior
for he has looked with favor on his lowly servant.
From this day all generations will call me blessed:
the Almighty has done great things for me,
and holy is his Name.
He has mercy on those who fear him
in every generation.
He has shown the strength of his arm,
he has scattered the proud in their conceit.
He has cast down the mighty from their thrones,
and has lifted up the lowly.
He has filled the hungry with good things,
and the rich he has sent away empty.
He has come to the help of his servant Israel
for he has remembered his promise of mercy,
the promise he made to our fathers,
to Abraham and his children for ever.[16]

Intercessions

Family members next can share their prayer intentions. After each spoken concern, the family says:

Lord, hear our prayer.

When all have had a chance to pray, the family prays together:

Our Father, who art in heaven,
hallowed be thy name;
thy kingdom come;
thy will be done
on earth as it is in heaven.
Give us this day our daily bread;
and forgive us our trespasses
as we forgive those who trespass against us;
and lead us not into temptation,
but deliver us from evil.
Amen.

Closing Prayer and Blessing

Evening Prayer ends by praying together:

Father of love,
hear our prayers.
Help us to know your will
and to do it with courage and faith.
Grant this through our Lord Jesus Christ, your Son,
who lives and reigns with you and the Holy Spirit,
one God, for ever and ever.

The leader says, as all make the sign of the cross:

May the Lord bless us,
protect us from all evil
and bring us to everlasting life.
—Amen.[17]

The Examen: Reviewing Your Day

Part of the rich tradition of the Catholic Church is recognizing the need to reflect on the day's activities—to remember God's invitation and our response (or lack of response). Saint Ignatius of Loyola developed a simple method by which you can review each day in a way that will help you grow in self-understanding and free you to follow God's will. This practice is called the Daily Examen. Your family can practice this prayerful review of the day before going to bed. Slowly read aloud these five steps as you relax in your favorite prayer place:

Stillness: Recalling God's Presence

Be aware of how God shows his love for you in all his gifts to you. Be thankful as you think of the love of God the Father, the love of his Son, Jesus, and the guidance of the Holy Spirit. Ask the Holy Spirit to come into your heart to help you look honestly at your actions this day and how you have responded in different situations. With the Holy Spirit's help, you can see what draws you close to God as well as what pulls you away from God.

Gratitude: Expressing Thankfulness

Review your day and give thanks to God for his gifts. Try not to choose what to be thankful for; instead, see what comes to mind. Think of the concrete details of your day—the smell of a rosebush in bloom, a smile from a friend, or a beautiful sunset. Recall the gifts God has given you that you can share with others—your ability to be helpful, your sense of humor, or your patience. Pause and express your thanks to the Father, the Son, and the Holy Spirit.

Reflection: Looking Back on Your Day

Again review the events of the day and notice how you acted in each situation. Recall your feelings and motives to see whether you freely followed God's will. Ask yourself when you were conscious of God's presence. Think about opportunities you had to grow in faith, hope, and charity. When we think about why we did or did not take advantage of these opportunities, we can become aware of how we might change our actions. Be grateful for the occasions when you freely chose to help others. Perhaps you let someone go ahead of you in line, or you kept a hurtful comment to yourself. These are examples of responding freely as God wants us to. When we think about the times we did or didn't act with God's grace, we can see ways to make a good response a habit.

Sorrow: Asking for Forgiveness

After you have asked for the Holy Spirit's help to reflect on the actions of the day, spend time talking with God. Express sorrow for the times you failed to follow his direction and ask him to be with you the next time. Give thanks to God for the grace that helped you to follow his will freely. Feel the sorrow and gratitude in your heart as you talk with God.

Hopefulness: Resolving to Grow

Ask God to help you as you look forward to a new day. Plan to follow and trust in the loving guidance of the Father, the Son, and the Holy Spirit. Conclude the day's prayerful review with the Lord's Prayer.

six

PRAYERS FOR SPECIAL SEASONS

CATHOLIC WORSHIP AND CELEBRATION FOLLOW A YEARLY CYCLE KNOWN AS THE LITURGICAL YEAR. Catholics—along with many other Christians around the world—follow this seasonal calendar by observing Advent, Christmas, Lent, Easter, and Ordinary Time. Much can be done at home to connect family prayer with the prayer cycle of the church. Because holy days and holidays frequently coincide, these are particularly good times to create family prayer traditions.

Put candles, flowers, or decorative cloths in a space your family likes to pray, and change the colors to match the seasons: violet for Advent, white for Christmas, violet for Lent, white for Easter, red for Pentecost, and green for Ordinary Time. Use prayer models to help celebrate the seasons of the Church year. Here are just a few suggestions.

Advent

The liturgical year begins with Advent, a word derived from Latin that means "coming." The Advent season includes the four weeks before Christmas beginning with the Sunday on or closest to November 30 and ending Christmas Eve. During Advent we prepare to celebrate the birth of Christ, and we look forward to Christ's second coming at the end of time. The liturgical color for Advent is violet.

The Advent Wreath

The Advent wreath is a popular family devotion for this season. It is usually a circle of evergreen branches surrounding four candles, one for each of the Sundays of Advent. Frequently, three of the candles are violet and one is rose. The rose-colored candle is lit during the third week of Advent beginning on Gaudete Sunday (*gaudete* means "joyful") as a reminder that our waiting will soon be over.

The Advent wreath is blessed on the first Sunday of Advent. One candle is lit the first week, two the second week, three the third week, and all four the fourth week. The prayer text for each week comes from the opening prayer for that Sunday's Mass. An Advent hymn and scripture reading may be included. For younger children, the prayers for each week may be simplified. Here is a good Advent prayer for all ages.

Come, Lord Jesus, we are waiting for your birthday.

Blessing the Advent Wreath

On the first Sunday of Advent, gather the family and bless the Advent wreath. Begin by making the sign of the cross.

Our help is in the name of the Lord.

Who made heaven and earth.

Reading

The people who walked in darkness
have seen a great light;
those who lived in a land of deep darkness—
on them light has shined.
You have multiplied the nation,
you have increased its joy;
they rejoice before you
as with joy at the harvest,
as people exult when dividing plunder.
For a child has been born for us,
a son given to us;
authority rests upon his shoulders;
and he is named

Wonderful Counselor, Mighty God,
Everlasting Father, Prince of Peace.
His authority shall grow continually,
and there shall be endless peace
for the throne of David and his kingdom.
He will establish and uphold it
with justice and with righteousness
from this time onwards and for evermore.
The zeal of the Lord of hosts will do this.

Isaiah 9:2–3, 6–7

Blessing

A parent leads the family in one of these blessings, or the family prays it in unison.

Loving God,
Our hearts desire the warmth of your love
And our minds are searching for the light of your Word.
As we light the candles of this wreath
Increase our longing for Christ our Savior
And give us the strength to grow in faith.
At the day of his coming may we be found
Prepared and filled with joy.
We ask this through Christ our Lord.
Amen.

Or the family prays:

Blessed are you, O Lord our God, king of the universe.
You sent your Son to be the Light of the world and to
    spread his light of love to all.
As we light the candles of this wreath
May its growing brightness remind us of the approaching
    nearness of your Son
So that the day of His coming may find us prepared and
    filled with joy.
We ask this through Christ our Lord.
Amen.

The First Week of Advent

This ceremony is meant for every day during the first week of Advent, beginning with the first Sunday.[18] Dinner and bedtime are made even more special with this ritual. The family prays one of these prayers as the first candle is lighted.

All-powerful God,
increase our strength of will for doing good
that Christ may find an eager welcome at his coming
and call us to his side in the kingdom of heaven,
where he lives and reigns with you and the Holy
*   Spirit,*
one God, for ever and ever.
Amen.

Or the family prays:

Father in heaven,
our hearts desire the warmth of your love,
and our minds are searching for the light of your
*   Word.*

Increase our longing for Christ our Savior
and give us the strength to grow in love,
that the dawn of his coming may find us rejoicing in
    his presence
and welcoming the light of his truth.
We ask this in the name of Jesus the Lord.
Amen.

The Second Week of Advent

The family prays one of these prayers as two candles are lighted each day.

God of power and mercy,
open our hearts in welcome.
Remove the things that hinder us from receiving
    Christ with joy,
so that we may share his wisdom
and become one with him
when he comes in glory,
for he lives and reigns with you and the Holy Spirit,
one God, for ever and ever.
Amen.

Or the family prays:

Father in heaven,
the day draws near when the glory of your Son
will make radiant the night of the waiting world.
May the lure of greed not impede us from the joy
which moves the hearts of those who seek him.
May the darkness not blind us
to the vision of wisdom
which fills the minds of those who find him.
We ask this in the name of Jesus the Lord.
Amen.

The Third Week of Advent

The family prays one of these prayers as three candles, including the rose-colored one, are lighted each day.

Lord God,
may we, your people,
who look forward to the birthday of Christ,
experience the joy of salvation
and celebrate that feast with love and thanksgiving.
We ask this through our Lord Jesus Christ, your Son,
who lives and reigns with you and the Holy Spirit,
one God, for ever and ever.
Amen.

Or the family prays:

Father of our Lord Jesus Christ,
ever faithful to your promises
and ever close to your Church:
the earth rejoices in hope of the Savior's coming
and looks forward with longing
to his return at the end of time.
Prepare our hearts and remove the sadness
that hinders us from feeling the joy and hope
which his presence will bestow,
for he is Lord for ever and ever.
Amen.

The Fourth Week of Advent

The family prays one of these prayers as all four candles are lighted.

Lord,
fill our hearts with your love,
and as you revealed to us by an angel
the coming of your Son as man,
so lead us through his suffering and death
to the glory of his resurrection,
for he lives and reigns with you and the Holy Spirit,
one God, for ever and ever.
Amen.

Or the family prays:

Father, all-powerful God,
your eternal Word took flesh on our earth
when the Virgin Mary placed her life
at the service of your plan.
Lift our minds in watchful hope
to hear the voice which announces his glory,
and open our minds to receive the Spirit
who prepares us for his coming.
We ask this through Christ our Lord.
Amen.

Christmas

Christmas, the memorial of Christ's birth, is celebrated December 25. Christmas is also a full liturgical season extending from the vigil of Christmas (Christmas Eve) to the Feast of the Baptism of the Lord, celebrated the Sunday after January 6. Included within the Christmas season are many celebrations that recall the early life of Jesus:

- the Feast of the Holy Innocents (December 28)
- the Feast of the Holy Family (the Sunday after Christmas)
- the Solemnity of Mary, Mother of God (January 1)
- the Solemnity of Epiphany (January 6, or the Sunday occurring between January 2 and 8)

The liturgical color for the Christmas season is white.

Here are some Christmas traditions you may want to use in your family's prayer time.

Blessing the Christmas Manger

St. Francis of Assisi introduced the custom of displaying the Christmas manger, also called the Nativity scene or crèche. If you have a Christmas manger in your home, you may wish to bless it. Some families set up the Nativity scene on Christmas Eve. Others set it up earlier in Advent but do not put the infant Jesus in the manger until Christmas Eve or Christmas Day.

Gather the family around the Christmas manger and make the sign of the cross.

LEADER:

Our help is in the name of the Lord.

ALL:

Who made heaven and earth.

Reading

In those days a decree went out from Emperor Augustus that all the world should be registered. This was the first registration and was taken while Quirinius was governor of Syria. All went to their own towns to be registered. Joseph also went from the town of Nazareth in Galilee to Judea, to the city of David called Bethlehem, because he was descended from the house and family of David. He went to be registered with Mary, to whom he was engaged and who was expecting a child. While they were there, the time came for her to deliver her child. And she gave birth to her firstborn son and wrapped him in bands of cloth, and laid him in a manger, because there was no place for them in the inn.

LUKE 2:1–7

Blessing Prayer

A parent leads, or the family prays in unison.

God of all creation,
From the beginning you have shown your love for us,
Attentive to our every need.
When the time came to send a savior you sent your Son to
be born of the virgin Mary and to bring us your justice,
*   peace, mercy, and love.*
Lord,
As we reflect upon Jesus' humble birth in a stable
We give you thanks for him,
Who is God-with-us and Savior of all who lives and reigns
*   for ever and ever.*
Amen.

Blessing the Christmas Tree

Traditionally, families set up the Christmas tree on Christmas Eve and kept it up until the Solemnity of Epiphany. It was a festivity that belonged to the Christmas season, not to Advent. If your family prefers to decorate the tree earlier, you might try waiting to turn on the tree lights until after the prayer of blessing on Christmas Eve.

Gather the family around the Christmas tree and make the sign of the cross.

LEADER:

Blessed be the name of the Lord.

ALL:

Now and for ever.

Reading

In the beginning was the Word, and the Word was with God, and the Word was God. He was in the beginning with God. All things came into being through him, and without him not one thing came into being. What has come into being in him was life, and the life was the light of all people. The light shines in the darkness, and the darkness did not overcome it.

JOHN 1:1–5

Blessing Prayer

A parent leads, or the family prays one of these prayers in unison.

Loving God,
We give you thanks for the care with which you have
*   created each of us and all of creation.*
We praise you for the sun and moon that give us light,
For the Law and the prophets that light our path so we
*   can walk in your ways,*
And for your son, Jesus Christ, whom you sent as light of
*   the world.*
Bless us as we light this tree.
May its light be a sign of the joy that fills us as we
*   celebrate the coming of your Son.*
May all who look upon this tree come to the knowledge
*   and joy of salvation.*
We ask this through Christ our Lord.
Amen.

Or the family prays:

Holy God, we celebrate the birth of your Son with great
joy.
He rescued us from the darkness of sin by making the tree
of the cross the means of our salvation.
May the splendor of this tree remind us of the life-giving
cross of Christ,
That we may always rejoice in the new life that shines in
our hearts.
We ask this through Christ our Lord.
Amen.

Light the Christmas tree. Sing Christmas hymns and carols. Keep the feast. Christ is born!

Lent

Lent is the name given to the time of preparation for Easter, lasting forty days in honor of Christ's forty-day temptation in the wilderness. Lent begins on Ash Wednesday, when the sign of the cross is traced on our foreheads in ashes. The ashes remind us of our origin and our death. (Thus the prayer when we receive ashes: "Remember that you are dust, and to dust you shall return.") The cross is also a sign of the victory over death that Christ won for us. We acknowledge that when we "[t]urn away from sin and [are] faithful to the gospel"—the other prayer you might hear when you receive ashes.

Lent lasts six weeks. The sixth Sunday is called Passion or Palm Sunday; it commemorates Jesus' entrance into Jerusalem and marks the beginning of Holy Week. Lent ends on Holy Thursday, when we recall Jesus' Last Supper with his apostles. We reach the high point of the entire liturgical year with the Triduum, the three days of Holy Thursday, Good Friday, and Holy Saturday, our "Passover" celebration of Jesus' death and resurrection.

The themes of Lent include both penance and baptism, as we recall Christ's suffering and journey with those preparing for initiation into the Church. During this season, the word "alleluia" is not said during Mass or in Catholic prayer. "Alleluia!" will return as the refrain of praise at Easter and throughout the Easter season.

The Jesus Prayer, beloved by Christians in the East, is an excellent prayer for the whole family to say throughout Lent. Pray it together in the morning before you go your separate ways or add it to another prayer you say later in the day.

Lord Jesus Christ,
Son of God,
have mercy on me,
a sinner.

Praying by Our Actions

During Lent, the Church calls us to penance—sorrow for our sins. Several traditional practices help us to repent.

- Fasting and abstinence on Ash Wednesday and Good Friday
- Abstaining from meat on Fridays during Lent
- Celebrating the Sacrament of Reconciliation
- Almsgiving: sharing our material resources with the poor

We limit the amount we eat for a period of time to express sorrow for sin and to make ourselves more aware of our hunger for God and of his action in our lives. Adults eighteen years old and older fast on Ash Wednesday and Good Friday. The practice is also encouraged as a private devotion at other times. Fasting means that we eat only one full meatless meal and two smaller meals with no snacking.

Abstinence means that we eat no meat (including poultry) or meat byproducts. We observe abstinence from meat on Ash Wednesday and all Fridays of Lent. This regulation applies to all Catholics over the age of fourteen. People who are ill or have particular medical conditions and women who are pregnant are not obligated to observe the regulations on abstinence and fasting. They are encouraged to pray, to do penance, and to help the less fortunate as a sign of their repentance and sorrow.

Many Catholics practice a voluntary fast during Lent by giving up something they normally enjoy. Families can decide together on additional practices, such as giving up television one night of the week. Or they might decide to forgo eating out and give the money they would have spent to charitable organizations, such as Catholic Relief Services' Operation Rice Bowl. During Lent, families can be especially attentive to their prayer times, perhaps adding reading scripture to their daily routines.

All of these practices are meant to remind us of our need for God's forgiveness and to lead us to greater joy in the Christian life.

Act of Contrition

Lent is the time of year for searching our souls, feeling sorrow for our sins, asking forgiveness of God and those we have hurt, and determining to do better. It is a wonderful time to celebrate the Sacrament of Reconciliation.

There are many ways we sin against God and one another, and there are many ways we can ask God and one another for forgiveness. It's a skill first learned at home.

An Act of Contrition is a prayer in which we confess our sinfulness to God and ask for God's forgiveness. Catholics are encouraged to pray an Act of Contrition every day. We also pray an Act of Contrition as part of the Sacrament of Reconciliation. Here is a traditional example.

My God,
I am sorry for my sins with all my heart.
In choosing to do wrong
and failing to do good,
I have sinned against you
whom I should love above all things.
I firmly intend, with your help,
to do penance,

to sin no more,
and to avoid whatever leads me to sin.
Our Savior Jesus Christ
suffered and died for us.
In his name, my God, have mercy.[19]

The Stations of the Cross

This popular devotion recalls the events of Christ's last day. It is believed to be based on the visits made by pilgrims to the Holy Land who walked the route Christ followed on his way to death. Pictorial representations for each station can be found in almost all Catholic churches. These stations provide a visual aid for praying this devotion; however, stations are not necessary. It is particularly popular to pray the Stations of the Cross during Lent, especially on Fridays in commemoration of Christ's death on that day of the week. At home, your family can mimic the pilgrims by adding movement to your prayer—alternately sitting and standing, or praying as you take a walk.

The following is a list of the Stations of the Cross with short scripture passages. Not all the stations can be found in the Passion stories of the Gospels; some are based on Catholic tradition.

First Station:
Jesus is condemned to death

Then the people as a whole answered, "His blood be on us and on our children!" So . . . after flogging Jesus, [Pilate] handed him over to be crucified.

MATTHEW 27:25–26

Second Station:
Jesus accepts his cross

After mocking him, [the soldiers of the governor] stripped him of the robe and put his own clothes on him. Then they led him away to crucify him.

MATTHEW 27:31

Third Station:
Jesus falls the first time

I gave my back to those who struck me, and my cheeks to those who pulled out the beard; I did not hide my face from insult and spitting.

ISAIAH 50:6

Fourth Station:
Jesus meets his mother

Simeon blessed them and said to his mother Mary, "This child is destined for the falling and the rising of many in Israel, and to be a sign that will be opposed so that the inner thoughts of many will be revealed—and a sword will pierce your own soul too."

LUKE 2:34–35

Fifth Station:
Simon helps Jesus carry the cross

As they went out, they came upon a man from Cyrene named Simon; they compelled this man to carry his cross.

MATTHEW 27:32

Sixth Station:
Veronica wipes the face of Jesus

And the soldiers wove a crown of thorns and put it on his head, and they dressed him in a purple robe. They kept coming up to him, saying, "Hail, King of the Jews!" and striking him on the face.

JOHN 19:2–3

Seventh Station:
Jesus falls the second time

Surely he has borne our infirmities and carried our diseases; yet we accounted him stricken, struck down by God, and afflicted.

ISAIAH 53:4

Eighth Station:
Jesus speaks to the weeping women

"Daughters of Jerusalem, do not weep for me, but weep for yourselves and for your children."

LUKE 23:28

Ninth Station:
Jesus falls the third time

But he was wounded for our transgressions, crushed for our iniquities; upon him was the punishment that made us whole.

ISAIAH 53:5

Tenth Station:
Jesus is stripped of his garments

They stare and gloat over me; they divide my clothes among themselves, and for my clothing they cast lots.

Psalm 22:17–18

Eleventh Station:
Jesus is nailed to the cross

Then Jesus said, "Father, forgive them; for they do not know what they are doing."

Luke 23:34

Twelfth Station:
Jesus dies on the cross

Then Jesus cried again with a loud voice and breathed his last.

Matthew 27:50

Thirteenth Station:
Jesus is taken down from the cross

After these things, Joseph of Arimathea, who was a disciple of Jesus, though a secret one, . . . asked Pilate to let him take away the body of Jesus. Pilate gave him permission; so he came and removed his body.

JOHN 19:38

Fourteenth Station:
Jesus is buried

Joseph took the body and wrapped it in a clean linen cloth and laid it in his own new tomb, which he had hewn in the rock. He then rolled a great stone to the door of the tomb and went away.

MATTHEW 27:59–60

Epilogue: The Resurrection

Was it not necessary that the Messiah should suffer these things and then enter into his glory?

LUKE 24:26

Easter Triduum

Between Lent and Easter Sunday lie the three most important days in the church calendar. These are Holy Thursday, Good Friday, and Holy Saturday. On these three days the Church gathers to commemorate the passion (suffering), death, and resurrection of Jesus.

On Holy Thursday, we celebrate the Mass of the Lord's Supper, during which we recall Jesus' Last Supper with his disciples and do as he did by washing one another's feet.

On Good Friday, we gather to commemorate the Lord's passion. This is the only day in the Church year when no Mass is celebrated. Instead, when we gather to venerate the cross, we share Eucharist that has been consecrated at Thursday's Mass of the Lord's Supper.

The Triduum culminates in the celebration of the Easter Vigil on Holy Saturday. We gather in darkness to await the resurrection of Christ. If there are adults and older children in the community who are to be baptized, their baptism, confirmation, and first Eucharist are celebrated at the Vigil. All of the faithful are encouraged to observe the Easter fast, which extends the Good Friday fast through Holy Saturday, until the Easter Vigil.

Families who choose to attend all the Easter Triduum services will experience the fullness of our Easter celebration. Families might also pray the Stations of the Cross on Good Friday. Then, at the Easter Vigil, the festivity begins. This spirit of joy can continue at home with a "break-the-fast" meal immediately after the vigil.

Easter

Easter is the most important feast day in the Church year. It is the day on which we celebrate Christ's resurrection from the dead. Like Christmas, Easter is both a day and a season. The season of Easter extends for fifty days, beginning on Easter Sunday and ending on Pentecost. The fortieth day after Easter is the Feast of the Ascension, a holy day of obligation commemorating when Jesus returned to his Father in heaven. Many dioceses in the United States celebrate the Ascension on the seventh Sunday of Easter.

Eastertide—all fifty days of it—is considered one great Sunday. The liturgical color for the Easter season is white. A good family prayer for Easter is the ancient exclamation of praise to God:

Alleluia!

Blessing of Food for the First Meal of Easter

For people who fast during Lent and especially during Good Friday and Holy Saturday, the first meal of Easter is especially welcome. Thus it has become customary to bless this meal in a special way. Here is a suggestion for celebrating this ritual.

LEADER:
Christ is risen. Alleluia.
ALL:
He is risen indeed. Alleluia.

Reading

Now on that same day two of them were going to a village called Emmaus, about seven miles from Jerusalem, and talking with each other about all these things that had happened. While they were talking and discussing, Jesus himself came near and went with them, but their eyes were kept from recognizing him. And he said to them, "What are you discussing with each other while you walk along?" They stood still, looking sad. Then one of them, whose name was Cleopas, answered him, "Are you the only stranger in Jerusalem who does not know the things that have taken place there in these days?" He asked them, "What things?" They replied, "The things about Jesus of Nazareth, who was a prophet mighty in deed and word before God and all the people, and how our chief priests and leaders handed him over to be condemned to death and crucified him. But we had hoped that he was the one to redeem Israel. Yes, and besides all this, it is now the third day since these things took place. Moreover, some women of our group astounded us. They were at the tomb early this morning, and when they did not find his body there, they came back and told us that they had indeed seen a vision of angels who said that he was alive. Some of those who were with us went to the tomb and found it just as the women had said; but they did not see him." Then he said to them, "Oh, how foolish you are, and how slow of heart to believe all that the prophets have declared! Was it not necessary that the Messiah should suffer these things and then enter into his glory?" Then beginning with Moses and all the prophets, he interpreted to them the things about himself in all the scriptures.

As they came near the village to which they were going, he walked ahead as if he were going on. But they urged him strongly, saying, "Stay with us, because it is almost evening and the day is now nearly over." So he went in to stay with them. When he was at the table with them, he took bread, blessed and broke it, and gave it to them. Then their eyes were opened, and they recognized him; and he vanished from their sight. They said to each other, "Were not our hearts burning within us while he was talking to us on the road, while he was opening the scriptures to us?" That same hour they got up and returned to Jerusalem; and they found the eleven and their companions gathered together. They were saying, "The Lord has risen indeed, and he has appeared to Simon!" Then they told what had happened on the road, and how he had been made known to them in the breaking of the bread.

LUKE 24:13–35

Blessing Prayer

A parent can lead this prayer, or the family can pray in unison.

Loving God,
We have received new life through the victory of your son
over sin and death.
Bless us and the food of this our Easter meal
May we who gather at the Lord's table
Continue to celebrate with family and friends at this table
And be admitted finally to the eternal banquet in heaven.
Grant this through Christ our Lord.
Amen.

Prayer during the Easter Season

Easter, like Lent, is a time for prayer. In Lent we searched our souls and prayed for God's mercy. Now in Eastertide we rejoice and praise God. This is a wonderful season to begin following the weekday cycle of readings for Mass. Families can gather throughout the fifty days of the Easter season to read scripture and pray joyful alleluias. Here are some praises designated for the Monday following Easter Sunday.

The Lord has risen from the dead, as he foretold. Let there be happiness and rejoicing, for he is our King for ever. Alleluia!
This is the day the Lord has made; let us rejoice and be glad. Alleluia!
Christ now raised from the dead will never die again; death no longer has power over him. Alleluia!

Ordinary Time

Ordinary Time is the rest of the year—the time when no particular aspect of Christ's life is being celebrated. There is a period of Ordinary Time after the Christmas season and before Lent, and another, longer period after Pentecost until Advent. The liturgical color for Ordinary Time is green.

Ordinary Time is an ideal time for ordinary prayers. It is a good time to begin observing Morning and Evening Prayer. Here is a little prayer by the thirteenth-century saint Richard of Chichester, whose words inspired the *Godspell* song "Day by Day."

Thanks be to you, O Lord Jesus Christ, for all the benefits you have given us,
and for all the pains and insults you have borne for us.
O most merciful redeemer, friend, and brother,
may we know you more clearly,
love you more dearly,
and follow you more nearly;
for your own sake.
Amen.

seven

Devotions to Mary

The Catholic Church has always given Mary a place of special reverence. Not only is she honored as Mother of God, she is also called Mother of the Church and therefore Mother of us all. We look up to her as a model of faith, humility, and courage, especially for saying yes to God's call in the face of uncertainty and persecution.

Because of the many traditions of appearances by Mary and special miracles attributed to her, many cultures have particular devotions to Mary. She is honored as Our Lady of Guadalupe (Mexico), Our Lady of Czestochowa (Poland), Our Lady of Lourdes (France), and Our Lady of Fatima (Portugal).

Though we love and respect Mary, we do not worship her. Worship is reserved for the Trinity. Our devotion to Mary leads us to greater union with God. We can also pray to her as a wonderful example of a parent.

The Hail Mary

This popular Marian prayer is based on words spoken to Mary in the Gospel of Luke—those spoken by the angel at the Annunciation (when Mary learned of God's plan for her) and those spoken by Mary's relative Elizabeth at the Visitation (when a pregnant Mary went to stay with and help the also-pregnant Elizabeth). This prayer is prayed repeatedly in the Rosary, a meditative Marian devotion during which we reflect on the Glorious, Joyful, Sorrowful, and Luminous Mysteries of the life of Christ and of Mary.

Hail Mary, full of grace,
the Lord is with you.
Blessed are you among women,
and blessed is the fruit of your womb, Jesus.
Holy Mary, Mother of God,
pray for us sinners,
now and at the hour of our death.
Amen.

The Rosary

The Rosary is one of the most popular Catholic devotions. Its rhythmic repetition helps us focus our thoughts and become aware of God's presence. The four sets of Mysteries provide vivid imagery especially helpful to children in our meditation on the life of Christ and Mary. People who pray the Rosary—whether individually or with their family—say it is a powerful tool in their spiritual life.

A rosary is a chain of beads set in groups of ten, called decades. Each bead within the decade represents a Hail Mary, and each decade represents a Mystery to be meditated on while reciting the prayers. Each decade is framed by a large bead for the Lord's Prayer, and a space for the Doxology.

Most people select one of the four groups of five Mysteries and meditate on one Mystery for each of the five decades. Here is how to pray the Rosary:

Make the Sign of the Cross.

In the name of the Father,
and of the Son,
and of the Holy Spirit.
Amen.

While holding the crucifix of the rosary, recite the Apostles' Creed.

I believe in God, the Father almighty,
creator of heaven and earth.
I believe in Jesus Christ, his only Son, our Lord.
He was conceived by the power of the Holy Spirit
and born of the Virgin Mary.
He suffered and died under Pontius Pilate,
was crucified, died, and was buried.
He descended to the dead.
On the third day, he arose again.
He ascended into heaven,
and is seated at the right hand of the Father.
He will come again to judge the living and the
dead.
I believe in the Holy Spirit,
the holy catholic Church,
the communion of saints,
the forgiveness of sins,
the resurrection of the body,
and the life everlasting. Amen.

Move your fingers to the large bead next to the crucifix.
While holding it, say the Lord's Prayer.

Our Father, who art in heaven,
hallowed be thy name;
thy kingdom come;
thy will be done
on earth as it is in heaven.
Give us this day our daily bread;
and forgive us our trespasses
as we forgive those who trespass against us;
and lead us not into temptation,
but deliver us from evil.
Amen.

Grasp the first small bead and say a Hail Mary for the gift of faith. On the second small bead, say a Hail Mary for the gift of hope. And on the third small bead, say a Hail Mary for the gift of love.

Hail Mary, full of grace,
the Lord is with you.
Blessed are you among women,
and blessed is the fruit of your womb, Jesus.
Holy Mary, Mother of God,
pray for us sinners,
now and at the hour of our death.
Amen.

Slide your fingers to the space following the third small bead, and say the Doxology.

Glory be to the Father,
and to the Son,
and to the Holy Spirit.
As it was in the beginning,
is now, and ever shall be,
world without end.
Amen.

Slide your finger to the single bead where the circle begins, and say the Lord's Prayer. You will say the Lord's Prayer at the beginning of each decade, every time your fingers meet a single bead.

Our Father . . .

Now you are ready to begin the first decade. Announce the Mystery on which you will meditate. For example, if you are saying the Joyful Mysteries, you will announce: "The Annunciation." Allow your children to talk about and imagine this event.

Take each of the ten small beads in turn, each time saying a Hail Mary.

Hail Mary . . .

After the tenth bead, your fingers will encounter a space. Say the Doxology.

Glory be to the Father . . .

You have now completed the first decade and the first Mystery. Announce the second Mystery: "The Visitation."

Repeat the cycle until you have meditated on all five Mysteries. (If this sounds complicated, just remember that the large beads are for the Our Father, the small beads are for the Hail Mary, and the spaces are for the Glory Be to the Father.) Many people conclude by praying the Salve Regina:

Hail, holy Queen, Mother of mercy,
hail, our life, our sweetness, and our hope.
To you we cry, the children of Eve;
to you we send up our sighs,
mourning and weeping in this land of exile.
Turn, then, most gracious advocate,
your eyes of mercy toward us;
lead us home at last
and show us the blessed fruit of your womb, Jesus:
O clement, O loving, O sweet Virgin Mary. [20]

The Joyful Mysteries

Meditate on these scenes from the Gospels on Mondays and Saturdays.

The Annunciation

Luke 1:26–38

The Archangel Gabriel appears to the Virgin Mary and tells her she will bear a son. Mary responds, "Here am I, the servant of the Lord; let it be with me according to your word."

The Visitation

Luke 1:39–56

Mary visits her relative Elizabeth, who is pregnant with John the Baptist. Mary prays the Magnificat: "My soul magnifies the Lord . . ."

The Birth of
Our Lord

Luke 2:1–20; Matthew 1:18–25

Mary and Joseph travel to Bethlehem, where Mary gives birth to Jesus in a stable. Meanwhile angels appear to shepherds and sing, "Glory to God in the highest heaven, and on earth peace among those whom he favors!"

The Presentation of Jesus
in the Temple

Luke 2:22–38

Mary and Joseph take Jesus to the temple for the ritual purification. Anna praises God and Simeon gives thanks: "My eyes have seen your salvation, which you have prepared in the presence of all peoples."

The Finding of Jesus in the Temple

Luke 2:41–52

Returning to Galilee after Passover, Mary and Joseph lose sight of the twelve-year-old Jesus, who has stayed in Jerusalem to talk with the teachers. "Why were you searching for me?" he asks. "Did you not know that I must be in my Father's house?"

The Sorrowful Mysteries

Reflect on these events in Christ's life on Tuesdays and Fridays.

The Agony in the Garden

Matthew 26:36–56; Mark 14:32–52;
Luke 22:39–53; John 18:1–11

Knowing he will soon be killed, Jesus prays in great anguish while his disciples doze. Judas arrives with soldiers, who arrest Jesus.

The Scourging at the Pillar

Matthew 27:26; Mark 14:65; 15:15;
Luke 22:63–65; John 19:1

The soldiers strike Jesus, torment him, and spit on him. Pilate has Jesus flogged.

The Crowning of Thorns

Matthew 27:27–31; Mark 15:16–20; John 19:2–3

The soldiers make a crown of thorns and place it on Jesus' head. They dress him in a purple robe and make fun of him, calling him "King of the Jews."

The Carrying of the Cross

Matthew 27:32; Mark 15:21; Luke 23:26; John 19:16–17

Tradition says that Jesus attempted to carry his own cross but, weakened by loss of blood, stumbled under its weight. Simon of Cyrene is then asked to carry the cross for him.

The Crucifixion and Death of Jesus

Matthew 27:33–66; Mark 15:22–47; Luke 23:32–56; John 19:18–42

Jesus is nailed to his cross, which is planted in the ground between two crucified thieves. He dies within hours, forgiving those who crucified him. Nicodemus and Joseph of Arimathea take him down from the cross and bury him in Joseph's tomb.

The Glorious Mysteries

Rejoice in these triumphant moments on Wednesdays and Sundays.

The Resurrection

Matthew 28:1–10; Mark 16:1–13; Luke 24:1–49; John 20:1–29

Before daybreak Sunday morning, Jesus rises from the dead. He appears first to Mary Magdalene, then to Peter and John, the other disciples, and two followers on their way to Emmaus.

The Ascension

Matthew 28:16–20; Mark 16:19–20; Luke 24:50–53; Acts 1:6–11

While his disciples watch, Jesus leaves this earth and is received into heaven, promising power from the Holy Spirit. Angels tell the disciples that Jesus will return.

The Descent of the Holy Spirit

John 20:19–23; Acts 2:1–13

The disciples, along with Mary and other women, gather regularly for prayer. With the sound of a rushing wind and the appearance of flames like fire, the Holy Spirit comes upon the group, who begin speaking in foreign languages.

The Assumption of Mary into Heaven

Though scripture does not mention Mary's last days, tradition tells us she went to St. John's home near Ephesus. There are no relics of Mary and no burial site because, when she died, she was taken body and soul to heaven.

The Crowning of Mary as Queen of Heaven

Revelation 12:1

Mary is often likened to the woman in Revelation who is "clothed with the sun, with the moon under her feet, and on her head a crown of twelve stars."

The Luminous Mysteries
(Mysteries of Light)

The Baptism of Jesus in the River Jordan
Mark 1:9–13

John baptizes Jesus, and the Holy Spirit descends upon him like a dove. God proclaims that Jesus is his beloved Son.

The Wedding Feast at Cana
John 2:1–5, 7–12

At Mary's request, Jesus performs his first miracle, changing water into wine. This was considered the beginning of his ministry.

The Proclamation of the Kingdom of God
Matthew 4:12–25, 9:35, 11:2–6, 15:29–31; Mark 1:14–15, 29-34; Luke 4:14–21

Jesus calls all to conversion and service to the Kingdom. He travels through Galilee, healing the sick and proclaiming the good news.

The Transfiguration of Jesus

Mark 9:2–4, 7

On a mountaintop, Jesus is revealed in glory to Peter, James, and John. Elijah and Moses appear and are talking with Jesus, whose clothes become dazzling white. A voice says, "This is my Son, the Beloved; listen to him!"

The Institution of the Eucharist

1 Corinthians 11:23–26

Jesus offers his Body and Blood at the Last Supper. He tells his apostles to "do this in remembrance of me."

Queen of Heaven

The fourth Glorious Mystery of the Rosary celebrates Mary's assumption into heaven, and the fifth, her coronation. Thus one of the many titles given to Mary is "Queen of Heaven." Her queenship is celebrated August 22, one week after the Solemnity of the Assumption (when Mary, who was without sin, was taken body and soul into the glory of heaven.) This prayer was composed in the twelfth century.

ALL:

Queen of heaven, rejoice, alleluia.

    For Christ, your Son and Son of God,

    has risen as he said, alleluia.

    Pray to God for us, alleluia.

LEADER:

Rejoice and be glad, O Virgin Mary, alleluia.

ALL:

For the Lord has truly risen, alleluia.

LEADER:

Let us pray.

God of life,

you have given joy to the world

by the resurrection of your Son, our Lord

    Jesus Christ.

Through the prayers of his mother, the Virgin Mary,

bring us to the happiness of eternal life.

We ask this through Christ our Lord.

ALL:

Amen.[21]

The Memorare

The author of this intercessory prayer to Mary is unknown, though credit is traditionally given to St. Bernard of Clairvaux. It has been widely used for at least five hundred years.

Remember, most loving Virgin Mary,
never was it heard
that anyone who turned to you for help
was left unaided.

Inspired by this confidence,
though burdened by my sins,
I run to your protection
for you are my mother.

Mother of the Word of God,
do not despise my words of pleading
but be merciful and hear my prayer.
Amen.[22]

Family Favorites

A place for our favorite Scripture passages,
prayers, notes and quotes

....
....
....
....
....
....
....
....
....
....
....
....
....
....
....
....
....
....
....
....
....
....

The Angelus

This is traditionally prayed three times a day: in the early morning, at noon, and at the end of the workday. The bells of many Catholic churches still sound the Angelus as a reminder of the presence of Christ in our daily lives.

LEADER:

The angel of the Lord declared unto Mary,

ALL:

and she conceived of the Holy Spirit.

Hail Mary, full of grace

the Lord is with you.

Blessed are you among women,

and blessed is the fruit of your womb, Jesus.

Holy Mary, Mother of God,

pray for us sinners,

now and at the hour of our death.

Amen.

LEADER:

"I am the lowly servant of the Lord:

ALL:

let it be done to me according to your word."

Hail, Mary . . . (say the prayer)

LEADER:

And the Word became flesh

ALL:

and lived among us.

Hail, Mary . . . (say the prayer)

LEADER:

Pray for us, holy Mother of God,

ALL:

that we may become worthy of the promises of Christ.

LEADER:

Let us pray.

Lord,

fill our hearts with your grace:

once, through the message of an angel

you revealed to us the incarnation of your Son;

now, through his suffering and death

lead us to the glory of his resurrection.

We ask this through Christ our Lord.

ALL:

Amen.[23]

Hail, Holy Queen

In Latin this prayer is known as Salve Regina. The text was probably composed in the eleventh century by Hermann the Lame, a monk of Reichenau. It was frequently said as part of the Divine Office, the church's daily prayer.

Hail, holy Queen, Mother of mercy,
hail, our life, our sweetness, and our hope.
To you we cry, the children of Eve;
to you we send up our sighs,
mourning and weeping in this land of exile.
Turn, then, most gracious advocate,
your eyes of mercy toward us;
lead us home at last
and show us the blessed fruit of your womb, Jesus:
O clement, O loving, O sweet Virgin Mary.[24]

eight

THE COMMUNION OF SAINTS

THE CATHOLIC CHURCH HONORS HOLY MEN AND WOMEN, CALLED SAINTS, WHO ARE MODELS FOR US OF A CHRISTIAN LIFE. Though we worship only God, we venerate the saints, meaning we honor them and ask them to pray for us. We ask the saints to intercede for us before God, just as we might ask a friend or family member to pray for us when we have special needs. Scripture commands us to pray for one another (see, for example, James 5:13–18), and God often blesses us in response to prayers from our friends the saints.

Here are some favorite prayers to saints and by saints, as well as one on behalf of our deceased loved ones, who are also part of "the communion of saints"—all those who have been saved in Christ, both living here on earth and with God in eternity.

A Prayer to St. Joseph

St. Joseph, Mary's husband, is the patron saint of the universal Church, of workers, of fathers, and of the dying (among other things). Little is known about him beyond what is found in the Gospel accounts, primarily that he was a carpenter and of the family of David. St. Joseph's feast day is celebrated on March 19, and the Feast of St. Joseph the Worker is celebrated on May 1.

Most faithful guardian of Jesus and spouse of Mary,
you know the anguish of my heart and the
complexity of my problem.
Obtain for me the light of the Holy Spirit
and all the help I need to enable me at all times and
     in all things
to fulfill the will of God.
I choose you this day, in the presence of Jesus and Mary,
as my counsel, to direct me in all necessities.
Guide me as I trust in God to strengthen my heart
     during my earthly pilgrimage.
Amen.

St. Patrick's Breastplate

St. Patrick was a bishop and apostle to Ireland in the fifth century, and he is that country's patron saint today. He returned to Ireland to preach even after escaping imprisonment there and fleeing to his homeland of Scotland. His feast day is March 17.

Christ, be with me, Christ before me, Christ behind me,
Christ in me, Christ beneath me, Christ above me,
Christ on my right, Christ on my left,
Christ where I live, Christ where I sit, Christ where
    I arise,
Christ in the heart of every person who thinks of me,
Christ in the mouth of every person who speaks of me,
Christ in every eye that sees me,
Christ in every ear that hears me.
Salvation is of the Lord.
Salvation is of the Lord,
Salvation is of the Christ.
May your salvation, O Lord, be ever with us.

Family Favorites

A place for our favorite Scripture passages,
prayers, notes and quotes

....

....

....

....

....

....

....

....

....

....

....

....

....

....

....

....

....

....

....

....

Make Me an Instrument of Your Peace

St. Francis was born in the twelfth century in Assisi, Italy, and is the founder of the religious community that bears his name, the Franciscans. He is remembered for living simply, caring for the poor, creating the Christmas custom of Nativity scenes, repairing churches, and caring for animals. He is a patron saint of Italy (with St. Catherine of Siena) and of the environment. His feast day is October 4. This prayer is often attributed to him.

Lord, make me an instrument of your peace:
where there is hatred, let me sow love;
where there is injury, pardon;
where there is doubt, faith;
where there is despair, hope;
where there is darkness, light;
and where there is sadness, joy.

O Divine Master, grant that I may not so much seek
to be consoled as to console;
to be understood as to understand,
to be loved as to love.
For it is in giving that we receive,
it is in pardoning that we are pardoned,
and it is in dying that we are born to eternal life.
Amen.

A Prayer of St. Catherine of Siena

St. Catherine of Siena is known as a "Doctor of the Church" for her devout holiness and her illuminative scholarly writing on the faith. This fourteenth-century Dominican nun advised popes and wrote several great spiritual works. She is the patron saint of nursing and of Italy (with St. Francis of Assisi). Her feast day is April 29.

You, O God, are a fire that takes away the coldness,
illuminates the mind with its light,
and causes me to know your truth.
And I know that you are beauty and wisdom itself.
The food of the angels, you give yourself to us in the
fire of your love.

St. Ignatius's Suscipe

In the sixteenth century St. Ignatius of Loyola founded the religious community known as the Society of Jesus, or Jesuits. His manual for spiritual growth, *Spiritual Exercises,* is still widely used today. He is the patron saint of spiritual exercises and retreats; his feast day is July 31.

Take, Lord, and receive all my liberty,
my memory, my understanding
and my entire will,
All I have and call my own.

You have given all to me.
To you, Lord, I return it.

Everything is yours; do with it what you will.
Give me only your love and your grace,
That is enough for me.

A Prayer of St. Thérèse of Lisieux

Also known as the "Little Flower" and Thérèse of the Child Jesus, St. Thérèse of Lisieux was born in France in 1873. At fifteen, she became a Carmelite nun; she died of tuberculosis at the age of twenty-four before realizing her dream to transfer to a monastery in the missionary country of French Indochina. In her teaching, Thérèse focuses on how the ordinary events of life can be made extraordinary and holy. She is the patron saint of foreign missions; her feast day is October 1.

After earth's exile, I hope to go and enjoy you in the
    homeland,
but I do not want to lay up merits for heaven.
I want to work only for your love.
In the evening of this life,
I shall appear before you with empty hands,
for I do not ask you, Lord, to count my works.
All our justice is blemished in your eyes.
I wish, then, to be clothed in your own justice
and to receive from your love the eternal possession
    of yourself.[25]

A Prayer for the Dead

Our Christian belief does not view death as an ending. As we pray in the Mass for the Dead, "Lord, for your faithful people life is changed, not ended. When the body of our earthly dwelling lies in death we gain an everlasting dwelling place in heaven."[26] Because life is changed, not ended, we continue to have communion with all those who have gone before us in death. Our prayers for those who have died and their prayers for us are the way we celebrate this relationship.

The Catholic Church teaches that there are three states in which souls die, and three corresponding relations with God after death.

"Those who die in God's grace and friendship and are perfectly purified live for ever with Christ." These souls remain with God for ever in heaven.

"To die in mortal sin without repenting and accepting God's merciful love means remaining separated from him for ever by our own free choice. This state of definitive self-exclusion from communion with God and the blessed is called 'hell.'"

Finally, "all who die in God's grace and friendship, but still imperfectly purified, are indeed assured of their eternal salvation; but after death they undergo purification, so as to achieve the holiness necessary to enter the joy of heaven."[27] This final purification is named purgatory.

When we pray for the dead, we are praying for the souls of those in purgatory, that they may soon be with God in heaven.

Eternal rest grant to him [her], O Lord,
and let perpetual light shine upon him [her];
May his [her] soul and the souls of all the faithful
*   departed,*
through the mercy of God,
rest in peace.
Amen.

nine

Prayers of Praise

ALMOST EVERYBODY PRAYS AT CERTAIN TIMES. We pray when we're frightened or lonely, when we need something desperately, or when we want it very much. We pray when something big is happening in our lives—a new baby, a marriage, a death. And we pray when we are supremely happy.

Happy people often sing, and Christians do a lot of singing at church. *Eucharist*, after all, means "gratitude," and a psalm is a kind of song. Here are some model prayers of joy, praise, and thanksgiving.

A Thank-You Prayer

This short thank-you prayer can be said anytime, anywhere. In church, we say it like this:

Thanks be to God.
In everyday language, we might just say:

Thank you, Jesus.

Praise in Heaven

The Book of Revelation includes beautiful prayers of praise. In chapter 7, there is a picture of the Church in heaven—people and angels and mysterious creatures all singing praises to God, giving thanks that "the Lamb at the center of the throne will be their shepherd, and he will guide them to springs of the water of life, and God will wipe away every tear from their eyes." This is their song:

Salvation belongs to our God
who is seated on the throne, and to the Lamb!
Amen! Blessing and glory and wisdom
and thanksgiving and honor
and power and might
be to our God for ever and ever!
Amen.

REVELATION 7:10,12

Praise the Lord!

In this happy song, the whole world is praising God. Read it in unison or antiphonally, alternating lines. Let the children add names of other creatures that praise God!

Praise the Lord!
Praise the Lord from the heavens; praise him in the
    heights!
Praise him, all his angels; praise him, all his host!
Praise him, sun and moon; praise him, all you
    shining stars!
Praise him, you highest heavens, and you waters
    above the heavens!

Add other praises from the heavens.

Praise the Lord from the earth, you sea monsters and
    all deeps,
fire and hail; snow and frost, stormy wind fulfilling
    his command!
Mountains and all hills, fruit trees and all cedars!
Wild animals and all cattle,
creeping things and flying birds!

Add other praises from created things on earth.

Kings of the earth and all peoples, princes and all
    rulers of the earth!
Young men and women alike, old and young
    together!

Add other praises from human beings.

Let them praise the name of the Lord,
for his name alone is exalted;
his glory is above earth and heaven.
Praise the Lord!
FROM PSALM 148

NOTES

THE SCRIPTURE QUOTATIONS CONTAINED HEREIN ARE FROM THE NEW REVISED STANDARD VERSION BIBLE: CATHOLIC EDITION COPYRIGHT © 1993 AND 1989 BY THE DIVISION OF CHRISTIAN EDUCATION OF THE NATIONAL COUNCIL OF THE CHURCHES OF CHRIST IN THE U.S.A. Used by permission. All rights reserved.

Excerpts from the English translation of the *Catechism of the Catholic Church* for the United States of America Copyright © 1994, United States Catholic Conference, Inc.—Libreria Editrice Vaticana. English translation of the: *Catechism of the Catholic Church Modifications from the Editio Typica* Copyright © 1997, United States Catholic Conference, Inc.—Libreria Editrice Vaticana. Used with permission.

English translation of the *Gloria*, Nicene Creed, Apostles' Creed, *Sanctus*, Doxology, Canticle of

Zechariah, and Canticle of Mary by the International Consultation on English Texts.

1. *Catechism of the Catholic Church, Second Edition* (Washington, D.C.: USCCB Publishing, 2000), *2763*.

2. *A Book of Prayers* (1982), 46.

3. *A Book of Prayers, 6*.

4. *Book of Blessings* (Collegeville, Minnesota: The Liturgical Press, 1989), *190, 192*.

5. *Book of Blessings, 194*.

6. *Book of Blessings, 402*.

7. The prayers in this chapter are from *The Roman Missal* (New York: Catholic Book Publishing Co., 1973).

8. *Shorter Christian Prayer* (New York: Catholic Book Publishing Co., 1988), *30.*

9. *Shorter Christian Prayer, 43.*

10. *Shorter Christian Prayer, 44.*

11. This version of Luke 1:68–79 is from *The Liturgy of the Hours* (1974), *691–92.*

12. *Shorter Christian Prayer, 30.*

13. *Shorter Christian Prayer, 30.*

14. *Shorter Christian Prayer, 37.*

15. *Shorter Christian Prayer, 38.*

16. This version of Luke 1:46–55 is from *The Liturgy of the Hours, 696.*

17. *Shorter Christian Prayer, 34.*

18. The weekly Advent prayers are adapted from *The Roman Missal.*

19. *Rite of Penance* (Washington, DC: United States Catholic Conference, 1974), *45.*

20. *A Book of Prayers, 34.*

21. *A Book of Prayers, 37.*

22. *A Book of Prayers, 34.*

23. Concluding prayer from *A Book of Prayers*, 36.

24. *A Book of Prayers, 10.*

25. Adapted from *Story of a Soul*, tr. John Clarke, O.C.D. © 1975, 1976, 1996 by Washington Province of Discalced Carmelites, ICS Publications, 2131 Lincoln Road, N.E. Washington, DC 20002-1199 U.S.A.; www.icspublications.org, *277.*

26. Excerpt from Preface for Masses for the Dead from *The Roman Missal*.

27. *Catechism of the Catholic Church, Second Edition, 1023, 1033, 1030.*

Index of Prayers